D1044947

· LAWYERS ·

FROM THE EARLY YEARS OF PUNCH

• LAWYERS•

Legal Laughter

Special Edition for PAST TIMES® Oxford, England

Robinson Publishing Ltd.
7, Kensington Church Court
London W8 4SP

This edition published by arrangement with Punch Ltd.
copyright © Punch Limited 1998

*A CIP catalogue record of this book is available
from the British Library*

ISBN 1–84119–006–3

Design and computer page make up
Penny Mills
Printed and bound in the EC

CONTENTS

'Oh, sir, please sir, is this Chancery Lane?'
'It is.'
'Ah I knowed it was!'
'Then why did you ask?'
''Cos I wanted to have counsel's opinion!'

THE
• LAW STUDENT •

QUESTIONS AT THE EXAMINATION OF LEGAL
CANDIDATES FOR ADMISSION

Hilary Term, 1845

*As the questions are generally much the same, we sub-
join a selection from the questions at the recent
Examination, to which we have affixed answers for the
guidance of future candidates.*

Preliminary

1 Where and with whom did you serve your clerkship?

A With Mr Grab. Partly in his office, and partly in
Regent Street, Julien's Concerts, the Cider
Cellars, or the Cigar Divan.

2   Mention some of the principal lawbooks you
     have read and studied.

A   Hoyle's Laws of Whist, Cribbage etc. The Rules
     of the Cricket Club; ditto of the Jockey Club.

3   Have you attended any law lectures?

A   I have attended to many legal lectures, when I
     have been admonished by police magistrates for
     kicking up rows in the streets, pulling off knock-
     ers etc.

LONG VACATION
'Now then, Latitat, tuck in your six-and-eightpenny!'

HELPFUL HINTS TO YOUNG BARRISTERS
'Never miss a chance of ingratiating yourself with the jury,
even at the expense of the judge.'
(An opportunity often occurs after lunch.)

Common Law

4   What is a real action?

A   An action brought in earnest and not by way of
a joke.

Equity and Conveyancing

5   What are a bill and answer?

A   Ask my tailor.

6   How would you file a bill?
A   I don't know but would lay a case before a blacksmith.

7   What steps would you take to dissolve an injunction?

A   I would put it in some very hot water, and let it remain there until it was melted.

8   What are post-nuptial articles?
A   Children.

9   State the effect of marriage upon the will of a man?
A   It generally has the effect of depriving him of a will of his own.

10 A dies seised of real estate without issue, an intestate, leaving his grandfather and his mother, and a brother and a sister. Which of these is his heir?
A   Whichever you please, my dear sir.

'What do you mean—"Mind my own business"'

Criminal Law. Proceedings
before Justices of the Peace.

11 What is simple larceny?
A   Picking a pocket of a handkerchief, and leaving
    a purse of money behind.

12 What is grand larceny?
A   The income tax.

13 What is burglary, and state some of the requisites?

A   The requisites for burglary are generally, a jemmy, some skeleton keys, and a dark lantern.

14 What is a criminal information, and under what circumstances will it be granted?

A   When you ask a cabman his fare, and he informs you that it is about twice at much as he has any right to demand from you.

15 Has there been any, and what recent alteration in the course of proceeding in the Crown Office?

A   No, the clerks are as off-hand as they always used to be.

Counsel (in the course of an hour's oration): 'Gentlemen, you cannot close your eyes—my lord cannot close his—to this important fact!'

BY A LAW STUDENT
IN CHAMBERS

The days are gone when I used to seek
Refreshment and fun in Henley Week,
But now all that is a thing of the past,
The pace at the time was too good to last,
Farewell to the straws and the flannel shirts,
Farewell to house boats, launches, and flirts,
Farewell to the champagne cups and cigarettes,
To the gloves and sweet things lost in bets;
In chambers, alas! I sit and groan,
Slaving, and writing, and waiting alone.
On parchment and paper with pen and ink
I draw the draughts I cannot drink.
I'll see if my chief is here … I'll try …
He's off! To Henley? … hem! … So am I!!

A barrister is only invited to sit on the Bench when he has some considerable amount of standing at the Bar.

Young Thing (to her Counsel who has just won the day for her): 'Oh, do give me a lock of your curly hair, please.'

THE
• DIVORCE LAWS •

DIVORCE MADE EASY
[1886]

Dear Mr Punch

A writer in the *St James's Gazette,* dealing with the subject of the Divorce Laws, calmly proposes that in any revision of the code, which he strongly advocates, 'women should be placed on the same footing with men.' Such a pestilent heresy of course provoked correspondence, and, as I have made a careful study of the subject, I beg to submit to you, sir, a few reasonable grounds for divorce, which this reformer will, I hope, include in his precious revised code.

A man should be allowed to obtain a divorce from his wife on all or any of the following grounds:—

1   If he sees anyone he likes better than his wife.

2   If his mother-in-law comes too often.

3   If his wife's brother borrows money of him.

4   If she objects to his going to Paris without her.

5   If, knowing that he prefers the tops of the muffins at breakfast, she eats any of them.

Client: 'So, I said to them "I've tried to get a settlement by fair means and failed. You will now hear from my lawyer."'

'Now, gentlemen of the jury, I throw myself upon your impartial judgment as husbands and fathers, and I confidently ask, does the prisoner look like a man who would knock down and trample upon the wife of his bosom? Gentlemen, I have done!'

Counsel: 'The cross-examination did not seem to worry you at all. Have you had previous experience?'
Client: 'Three wives.'

6   If she hears him come in at four in the morn-
    ing, when he has considerately taken off his boots
    to do so quietly.

7   If she refers to it.

8   If she ever says, 'My dear, I think we have heard
    that story before.'

9   If she does not laugh consumedly whenever he
    tells a comic story.

PUNCH'S DICTIONARY

BAR GOLD. Fees to counsel.

DAMAGES. What a man gets by
going to law; and, as the word is
derived from *damnum,* is
exceedingly appropriate.

Lady Barrister: 'What is your age?'
Female Witness: 'About the same as yours, Madam.'

10   If she objects to smoking.

11   If she is not civil to *all* his male friends.

12   And female ones.

Policeman at the Law Courts: 'Strict orders to-day, m'm, No one to be admitted unless they're in wig an'—that is—beg pardon m'm—barristers, m'm—only barristers!'

Bright young thing: 'I say, what a rotten lot of books you keep! Don't you read Edgar Wallace?'

There, sir, you have a dozen suggestions which I would commend to the attention of this law reformer. You will observe I have not included any *trivial* reasons for divorce, and the procedure, as the *St James's Gazette* says 'should be as expeditious and inexpensive as possible.'

Yours faithfully,

A Tender Husband,
Turtle Dove Terrace.

A judge who was trying a case in which the wife of the defendant confessed to having got thirty-six blouses and ten hats in eighteen months remarked that he himself only bought one hat a year. A lady points out that he was silent as to the number of blouses he purchased during the same period.

May 11th, 1904

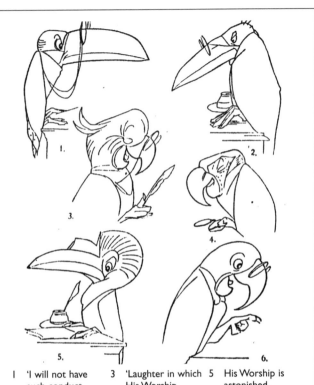

1	'I will not have such conduct. Clear the court.'	3 'Laughter in which His Worship joined.'	5 His Worship is astonished.
2	'Six months.'	4 'I think we have heard that tale before.	6 Dismissed with a caution.

UP BEFORE
· THE BEAK ·

CROSSED-EXAMINATION
[1892]

OLD STYLE

*Nervous Witness about to leave the box when his progress is
arrested by Counsel on the other side.*

COUNSEL *(sharply)*. No, sir, do you know the value of an
oath?

WITNESS *(taken aback)*. Why, yes—of course.

COUNSEL *(pointing at him)*. Come, no prevarication!
Do you understand the value, or do you not?

WITNESS *(confused)*. If you will allow me to explain—

COUNSEL. Come, sir, you surely can answer yes or no—
now which is it?

WITNESS. But you will not let me explain—

AT THE SESSIONS

Counsel: 'Do you know the nature of an oath my good woman?'

Witness (with a black eye): 'I did ought to, sir! Which my 'usban' is a Covin' Garden porter, sir!'

COUNSEL. Don't be impertinent, sir! Explanation is unneeded. Mind, you have been sworn, so if you *don't* know the value of an oath, it will be the worse for you.

WITNESS. But you won't let me speak.

'Always laugh at the judge's jokes. It is not upon such an occasion that his lordship observes that he *will* not have this court turned into a theatre.'

COUNSEL. Won't let you speak! Why, I can't get a word out of you. Now, sir, in plain English—are you a liar or not?

WITNESS (*appealing to Judge*). Surely, my lord, he has no right to speak to me like this?

JUDGE. Be good enough to answer the counsel's questions. I have nothing to do with it.

FOREMAN (*to Judge*). May we not ask, my lord, how you consider this case is being conducted.

Counsel calls the judge 'Mister.'

'I must ask you to withdraw that most sarcastic remark, Mr Jones.'
'I withdraw the remark, m'lud, but with your permission I should prefer the sarcasm to remain.'

JUDGE.   With pleasure, gentlemen! I will repeat what I remarked to the Master quite recently. I think the only word that will describe the matter is 'noble.' Distinctly noble!

[*Scene closes upon despair of Witness*]

NEW STYLE.

Arrogant witness about to leave the box, when his progress is arrested by Counsel on the other side.

COUNSEL. I presume, sir, that—

WITNESS (*sharply*). You have no right to presume. Ask me what you want, and have done with it.

COUNSEL (*amiably*). I think we shall get on better— more quickly—if you kindly attend my questions.

WITNESS. Think so? Well, it's a matter of opinion. But, as I have an engagement in another place, be good enough to ask what you are instructed to ask and settle the matter off hand.

COUNSEL. If you will allow me to speak—

WITNESS. Speak!—I like that! Why, I can't get a rational word of of you!

COUNSEL (*appealing to Judge*). Surely, my lord, he has no right to speak to me like this?

JUDGE. Be good enough to answer the witness. I have nothing to do with it.

WITNESS (*impatiently*). Now, sir, am I to wait all day?

COUNSEL (*mildly*). I really venture to suggest that that is not quite the tone to adopt.

These gentlemen are expected to be in a judicial frame of
mind after hanging about the precincts of the court for
several days, under penalty of a heavy fine, while their private
business in the city and elsewhere is going to the dogs.
(Why should not half-pay officers do the work, and
relieve busy men?)

WITNESS. Don't bully, me, sir! I am here to answer any
    questions you like to put, always supposing that
    you have any worth answering.
COUNSEL. But come—surely you ought to—
WITNESS. I am not here to learn my duty from you, sir.

'Show no mercy to the police; they have few friends.'

You don't know your subject, sir. How long have
you been called?

COUNSEL. I decline to reply.

JUDGE (*to Counsel*). Now you had really better be careful.
I wish to treat the Bar with every respect, but if you
waste any more time I shall feel strongly inclined to
bring your conduct before your benchers.

WITNESS. You hear what his lordship says. What are you
going to do next?

COUNSEL (*confused*). I don't know.

WITNESS (*to Jury*). He doesn't know! I needn't stay here any longer.

[*Stands down*]

JUDGE (*to Jury*). May I ask you, gentlemen, how you consider this case is being conducted?

FOREMAN OF THE JURY. With pleasure, my lord. We were all using the same word which exactly describes the situation. We consider the deportment of the witness 'noble.' Distinctly noble.

[*Scene closes upon despair of Counsel*]

MANNERS OF THE BAR
A sketch in the law courts, showing the patient and respectful attention of the counsel for the plaintiff during the speech of counsel for the defendant.

PROBABLY THE NEXT ABSURDITY
in ladies' winter costumes

34

LADIES
• AT THE BAR •

TO PORTIA
AT THE BAR

('The first lady barrister has just
taken the oath at Paris.'
— *Daily paper*).

[*c*1882]

O Portia, many maids there are,
　　Who wear their wigs as gaily
As thou, appearing at the bar
　　To take refreshers daily;
They rustle too, in silk like thee,
　　With oft a clerk resplendent
And, not infrequently you see,
　　Solicitors attendant.

Lady Solicitor: 'Why did you dissuade Miss Brown from bringing a Breach of Promise action against Tom Jones? She would have been sure to win it.'
Lady Barrister: 'Undoubtedly. But he is now engaged to me.'

Their trade is legal—so is thine,
    Yet not their craft thou pliest
For they are in the liquor line.
    And thou in law—the driest.
But welcome, bar maid! hail to thee!
    Bright be thy lot and griefless!
And may thy portion never be,
    Like this poor writer's, briefless.

NOVELTY IN COIFFURES
Suitable for ladies called to the bar.

COURTROOM
• DRAMAS •

THE LAW IN FILMLAND
[1925]

The law provides as much scope for energy as any profession in the State of Filmland. A barrister of any eminence finds his working hours crowded with divorce cases and murder trials; all of thrilling importance. Thanks too to the mental alertness of the Filmland judge and jury, he can construct a perfectly damning prosecution in a very few minutes by shaking his forefinger, slapping his papers and working his mouth in such a way as to cause everybody in court to look sombrely at one another and shake their heads. It is sheer bad luck that the case for the prosecution should so often be ruined by the appearance, at the moment of forensic triumph, of a missing witness, who arrives hatless and dishevelled from the customary cross-country race against time but full of beans and incontrovertible evidence in favour of the accused.

There is much less dull routine in the business round of a family solicitor in Filmland than in most countries. Whether you see him in his own comfortable office or in a client's ancestral library he is certain to be on the verge of making a dramatic and probably unpleasant disclosure. Yet, despite the rage and anguish he arouses in many a heaving bosom and throbbing shirt-front, he himself is

He can construct a perfectly damning prosecution in a very few minutes by shaking his forefinger.'

'It is true, me lud, that my client threw a bottle of wine at the defendant's head. But, I submit, me lud, that it was a very light wine, and, in fact, a wine that couldn't possibly hurt anybody.'

devoid of harshness or cynicism. In his genial old-fashioned way he rather enjoys causing trouble and strife, because be knows that in ten or twenty years' time he or his successor will discover a new will or some other important document which will bring happiness to all who really deserve it. It is this comforting assurance which enables the good old man, during the intervening years of intrigue and family feuds, to pocket his fees with a joyous heart.

BEHIND THE SCENES

First Judge: 'Breach of promise still running?'
Second Judge: 'Going wonderfully. No standing room.
What are you doing?'
First Judge: 'A building contract. Wretched business:
not a soul in the place!'

LAUGHED OUT OF COURT
[1905]

Although there is no real theatrical representation that is free in London, there is something that is equally good and that is Mr. Plowden's Court. From time to time managers have put on farces and comedies that have caused a certain amount of merriment—from *Our Boys* to *Charley's Aunt*—but their efforts have been trifling compared with those of London's Premier Jester, as Mr Plowden is called on the posters outside the Marylebone Court House, where he performs every morning. (Early doors open at 8.30.)

The Court being not too easy to find it will be well to take a cab, the cost of which, since you are so obviously from the country, will be about seven-and-six.

We will now enter the Court which you will notice is ventilated entirely by gusts of mirth and lighted by laughing gas. Observe the faces of the constables on duty, how deeply lined they are with the ravages of glee. Observe the Welkin; how it rings. Note the split sides of all the Court attendants.

How long you will be able to stand the Court depends

on your physique and capacity to see a joke. If you are Scotch you may last till lunch; otherwise you will collapse early. First aid to the amused having been administered by the Court's doctor, perhaps it would be as well to hasten to Kensal Green or Bunhill Fields for an antidote.

DULL MORNING IN MR. PLOWDEN'S COURT

THE
• BARRISTER •

BARCAROLES FOR
BRIEFLESS BARRISTERS
Air—"The Sea! the Sea!"

The fee! the fee! the welcome fee!
The new! the fresh! the scarce to me!
Without a brief, without a pound,
I travel the circuit round and round.
I draw with the pens at each assize,
If ink before me handy lies.
I've got a fee! I've got a fee!
I've got what I so seldom see;
With the judge above, and the usher below,
I wait upon the last back row.
Should a silk gown come with argument deep,
What matter! I can go to sleep.

A welcome case of judicial sympathy is reported from West London. It appears that a Society lady charged with shop-lifting pleaded that she was the sole support of two kennel-ridden poodles, and was immediately discharged.

March 3rd, 1920

I love (oh, how I love) to bide
At some fierce, foaming, senior's side.
When every mad word stuns the court,
And the judges wish he'd cut it short,
And tell him the case of So-and-So,
His argument doth to atoms blow.
I never hear Chancery's dull, tame jaw,
But I love the fun of the Common law,
And fly to the Exchequer; Bench and Pleas,
As a mouse flies back to a Cheshire cheese!
For the cheese it always seemed to me,
Especially if I got a fee!

My whiskers are white, my head is bald,
Since the dreary hour when I was call'd.
The Steward he whistled as out he told
The fees at my call from a packet of gold.
And never was heard of a step so wild
As took to the bar the briefless child.
I've liv'd since then, in term and out,
Some thirty years, or thereabout;
Without a brief, but power to range
From court to court by way of change.
And death, whenever he comes to me,
Will find me most likely without a fee.

The legal profession is suffering severely from the extraordinary but welcome decline in litigation

'That's right—one law for the rich and
half-a-dozen for the poor!'

THE JOLLY YOUNG
BARRISTER

And did you not hear of a jolly young barrister,
    At the Old Bailey who used for to ply?
He made out his case with such skill and dexterity
    Twisting each fact, while he glozed o'er each lie.
He stuck at nothing; and that so steadily,
The felons all sought his aid so readily,
And he saved from conviction so many a thief,
That this Barrister ne'er was in want of a brief.

What sights of fine rogues he got off by his
      blarney;
    His tongue was so glib, and so specious withal,
He was always retained by the great City forgers
    To Newgate from Mansion House sent, or
      Guildhall.
And often the Press would be gibing and jeering,
But 'twas all one to him, its carping and sneering;
He'd swear black was white in behalf of thief,
So this Barrister ne'er was in want of a brief.

And yet, only think what strange morals have
    lawyers,
    The Bar of such conduct think nothing at all;
Whilst should any poor Counsel report for a
paper,
    'To Coventry with him!'   that instant they call;
From their mess they'll expel him, he'll find to his
    sorrow;
But they'll dine with the housebreaker's hireling
    to-morrow;
Then hurrah!—though his client be swindler or
    thief—
For the Barrister never in want of a brief.

LEGAL INQUIRY — If I buy a pair of trousers warranted to wear well, and they turn out a failure, should I, on bringing an action for damages, be *"non-suited,"* or could I counterclaim damages for *"breeches of promise"*?

PUNCH'S DICTIONARY

BRIEF (IN LAW) A complicated account of a simple transaction. which enables Counsel to mystify himself and everybody else about an ordinary matter. Drawing a brief resembles the ingenious contrivance of Dido, who cut a bull's hide into strips on being assigned as much land as she could enclose with the hide of that animal. Thus in drawing a brief. facts are cut up into shreds and patches or torn to ribbons, for the purpose of rendering them so roundabout as to cover as much space of paper as possible.

THE BAR AND ITS MOANING

I am watching, I am waiting,
    And my hair is growing grey,
For it is exasperating,
      That no business comes my way.

Other men in briefs may revel
    When successfully they plead,
I am only a poor "devil,"
    Often worked but never fee'd.

E'en the bank-clerk in the city
      Has a salary that's small,
But we juniors, more's the pity,
    Don't make anything at all.

Living still on false pretences,
    Since the truth we dare not own,
Some not earning their expenses
    If the facts were truly known.

And meantime the years are flying,
    Bringing changes p'raps for some,
Not for me tho'; I'm relying
    On the practice that's to come.

Old Lady (at the Law Courts): 'Could you kindly direct me sir, to—'
Young Briefless: 'My Dear Madam, I'm a perfect stranger myself— don't think I've been in a court for the last twenty years!'

First Articled Clerk: 'Well, how did your private theatricals go off?'
Second Articled Clerk: 'Pretty well. My moustache went off at once, but nothing would induce the pistol to go off in the duel scene!'

IN
· CHAMBERS ·

THE BARRISTER'S CLERK
[1848]

Having now taken chambers all to myself, I found myself suddenly surrounded and beset by a parcel of boys of every age and of every style of British costume, who have been collected by an advertisement I caused to be inserted in the paper for a clerk. They were told to apply between one and two, but they were between forty and fifty at least, giving life and juvenility to the whole staircase by the playful gambols in which they indulged. Leap-frog was rampant in the passages; while marbles and peg-top made up with conversation the occupation of the pavement at the bottom of the stairs.

It would be uninteresting to describe my numerous interviews with the miscellaneous candidates for the single, and not very profitable clerkship I had to bestow.

Some of them to whom I proposed the 'half-crown' by way of salary, and who knew something of the probable proceeds of this mode of remuneration, asked me bitterly whether I wanted 'to starve a cove?' whereupon, not wishing to have that ponderous burden, a 'starved cove,' upon my conscience, I closed with an urchin not yet in his teens—except his trowsers, which were velveteens—for four shillings a week, and the usual clerical perquisites.

I was surprised to find, by the offers of the applicants, the very miscellaneous uses to which a barister's clerk could be applied. Some had been accepted to look after horses, as well as asses—I mean clients—and some twenty or thirty had no objection to undertaking the care of a cat.

The great majority were willing to clean my boots—in this I should have met them half-way, for I wore high-lows—and two or three had a little carpet-beating and new-laid egg connection, which they hoped their arrangements with me would not render it necessary to disturb. One drove a cab three days a week, and was willing to give me the benefit of his clerkship on the alternate days, with an undertaking not to wear corduroy breeches at chambers; and one juvenile who had been accustomed to deal in congreve matches, thought that his connection with the brimstone trade, and his dealings with Lucifer, would be considered to have qualified him for introduction to the law.

It was rather too bad, you know, that Larkins serving poor Jones like this! And his first circuit too!

RIGHT
• AND WRONG •

WHAT A BARRISTER MAY DO; AND
WHAT HE MAY NOT
[1845]

There seems to be at present a very considerable
difference of opinion among the gentlemen of the Bar as
to what may or may not be done by a barrister. We had
some idea of publishing a small hand-book of etiquette
for the exclusive use of the gentlemen of the long robe;
but as what is etiquette to-day may not be etiquette to-
morrow, we feared the work would not possess the
permanent utility which alone would recompense us for
the labour of writing it. We have, however, drawn up a
few general rules founded on our own observation as to
what a barrister may do, and what he may not do,
consistently with his professional dignity:—

PUNCH'S DICTIONARY

COUNSEL A Barrister, whose duty it is to manage the causes of his clients, and get rid of their effects. Some are called Common-law Counsels, to whom law is not common at all, for they are seldom employed; and there are also Chamber Counsels, who sit in their chambers, doing nothing, and so far deserve the name. Counsels are punishable for malpractice by being prohibited from addressing the Court; but that which prohibits Counsel from addressing the Court is not so much malpractice as no practice at all.

1st   A barrister may be employed in inducing Members of Parliament to vote in favour of railway bills; but he may not report for a newspaper.

2nd   A barrister may practise the 'artful dodge' for the purpose of defeating the ends of justice; but he must not enter an assize town in an omnibus.

'Then, of course, there'll be the usual search fee.'

Legal Adviser (speaking technically): 'In short you want to meet
your creditors.'
Innocent Client: 'Hang it no! Why they're the very people
I'm anxious to avoid!'

Aged Criminal (who has just got a life sentence): 'Oh, me lud,
I shall never live to do it!'
Judge (sweetly): 'Never mind. Do as much as
you can!'

3rd A barrister may tout for a small judgeship; but he will be very properly disbarred if he advertises his readiness to plead the cause of clients.

4th A barrister may libel a rival candidate for an office in a 'private and confidential' circular; but he must not degrade himself by asking an attorney to dine with him on the circuit.

Prisoner: 'Your Honour—'
Judge (drowsily): 'Is it? I thought you won the last hole.'

5th   A barrister may take a fee when he knows he cannot attend to the cause; but he may not return the money, for his doing so would be very unprofessional.

6th, and
lastly   A barrister may be a very honourable man; but many things which professional etiquette allows him to do, would be thought disgracefully dishonest among ordinary people.